A Note on Pronunciation

The Dutch name Jip is pronounced 'Yip'.

    Janneke is a little more difficult. It might be easiest to think of as 'Yannicka', with the A as in 'father' and a firm stress on the first syllable.

Annie M.G. Schmidt & Fiep Westendorp

A Year in Holland with Jip en Janneke

Translated by David Colmer

Amsterdam · Antwerpen
Em. Querido's Kinderboeken Uitgeverij
2017

Cold but Already Spring

'Oh,' says Mother. 'I don't have any flowers. The house looks so dull without them.'

'Shall we pick some?' asks Jip.

'I don't think there are any,' Mother says. 'It's still winter.'

But Jip calls out, 'Janneke!'

'Yes,' Janneke calls back. 'I'm coming.'

'Shall we go and pick some flowers?' Jip asks.

'Okay,' says Janneke.

And off they go. They go to the meadow.

But it's cold. And the grass is sopping wet. And there aren't any flowers. Only sheep.

'Aren't you cold?' Jip asks a sheep.

The sheep stares at him. But it doesn't say a word.

'They're not cold,' Janneke says. 'They've got thick woolly coats on. They're nice and warm.'

Then Jip and Janneke carry on. They go down the avenue. The avenue with all the big houses. Big houses with front gardens.

'Look,' Jip says. 'There's some flowers.' And he points at them.

Yes, there are some beautiful yellow flowers.

'But we're not allowed to pick them,' Janneke says. 'They're not ours. They belong to that lady.'

'I know,' Jip sighs. 'I wish we could.'

But the lady who lives in the house is sitting by the window. And she looks out and sees Jip and Janneke.

She comes outside.

And she says, 'Would you like a few branches? A few branches with little yellow flowers on them?'

'Yes, please,' say Jip and Janneke.

Then the lady fetches a knife. And she cuts off three branches. Really beautiful branches.

Jip and Janneke go home.

They are so happy.

'Look,' says Jip.

'Oh, Jip,' says Mother. 'What have you got there? How did you get them?'

'A lady gave them to us,' says Jip.

Mother puts the branches in a vase. And they look really lovely.

And Jip says, 'I'm going to go to that house every day now. And every day I'll get flowers.'

'Not at all,' says Mother. 'You mustn't do that. Soon we'll have flowers of our own. Just wait.'

And now Jip and Janneke are waiting for the flowers.

Painting Eggs

'Here,' says Mother. 'I've got a dozen eggs. I've boiled them. Six for Jip. And six for Janneke. Go and paint them.'

Jip and Janneke are sitting at the table. There's a big newspaper spread out on it. In case they make a mess. And they're wearing aprons. And they've got a little paintbrush each. And paint. Red and green and purple and blue and yellow.

'I'll do one to show you,' says Mother. 'Look, you can make a face on the egg. With eyes and a nose. And a hat.'

Jip tries to do it too. But the egg is so smooth. And so round. One eye ends up on top and other one on the bottom.

Janneke does an egg with stripes. And one with blobs. They turn out really well. Jip and Janneke work hard on the eggs.

And when Mother comes to have a look, she says, 'Ooh! Lovely!'

'They're finished!' Jip shouts. 'All of them!'

'And you two are beautifully painted too, I see,' says Mother.

Jip looks at Janneke.

'Ha-ha,' he yells. 'You're green and purple and blue.'

'So are you!' Janneke screams. 'You're yellow and red and black!'

'Look in the mirror,' Mother says.

And then Jip and Janneke climb up on a chair. In front of the mirror. And they can't stop laughing.

'You're two little Easter eggs yourselves,' says Mother.

Picking Flowers

It's springtime. And Jip's wearing yellow socks. As yellow as the crocuses. As yellow as the buttercups. And Janneke's legs are bare.

'We're going to go really far,' says Jip. 'We're going to go for a really long walk.'

'Not too far,' says Mother.

Off they go. 'First one to the willow tree,' says Jip. And he starts running. He runs really fast! And Janneke races along behind him. She can't go as fast as Jip. She's puffing. She calls out, 'Wait for me!' Jip is already in the meadow. Next to the willow. And he says, 'Beat you.'

'Shall we pick some flowers?' Janneke asks. 'I'll pick the daisies.'

'And I'll pick these ones,' Jip says, 'these yellow ones.'

'Ugh,' says Janneke. 'They're weeds. They're dandelions.'

'No, they're not,' Jip says. 'They're not dandelions. They're... They're...' He's not sure. 'They're roses. Yellow roses.'

'Ha-ha,' Janneke laughs. 'They're not roses, silly.'

Yes, they are, and Jip keeps picking them. Until there are none left. He can't see any more anywhere.

'There's another one,' Janneke cries. 'Next to the ditch.'

Aha. Jip sees them too. At least ten. He hurries over but there are stinging nettles there too. He has to be careful.

'Ow,' Jip shouts. 'Ow, ow...' He's brushed against the nettles. And he's really angry.

'Stupid stinging nettles,' he shouts. 'Nasty, stupid stinging nettles!'

And he stamps on them. Again and again. And then Jip takes a step back. And he's stepped straight into the ditch.

Oh no! Look at him now. With both feet in the water.

He's so shocked, he forgets to cry. Because of the fright. Thank goodness it's not deep.

'Quick,' Janneke says. 'Take my hand.'

And Janneke tugs and pulls.

Gloop, says the mud in the ditch. Phew, Jip's back up on dry land.

'Your socks,' says Janneke. 'Oh, your beautiful yellow socks. They're all filthy. They've turned green. Green from the duckweed.'

Jip and Janneke go home. And Mother says, 'What have you done now, Jip? Look at your shoes. And your socks.'

'It wasn't my fault,' says Jip.

'No, it wasn't his fault,' Janneke says. 'It was because of the dandelions.'

'They're not dandelions,' says Jip. 'Here, Mother, for you. Yellow roses.'

And Mother's so happy. She forgets all about the yellow socks.

Jip Rides a Bike

Here comes Father on his bike. He's home. Jip goes out to meet him. 'Here,' says Father, 'you can put the bike away, Jip.'

Jip is really pleased. He's allowed to take the bike around the back of the house. To put it in the shed.

'Be careful,' Father says. And Father goes inside.

Jip is still standing out on the street with the bike. And here comes Janneke.

'I'm going for a ride!' Jip says. 'Look, I can ride a bike.'

Janneke watches with wide eyes. And Jip sticks one leg through under the crossbar. He holds on tight to the handlebars. And he starts to pedal. It goes well. Oh, it's going so well. Jip really can ride a bike. He does wobble a bit. And he does zigzag. But he's turning the pedals and moving along.

'Wow!' Janneke shouts. She starts clap-

ping. 'Wow! Can I have a go?'

But Jip has lots more tricks to show her. Now he starts to steer to the left. He takes a corner. And then it happens! The bike falls over. With a bang.

'Ooh!' cries Janneke. Jip is lying on the ground with the bike on top of him. He's completely covered by the bike. What a terrible accident. How terrible.

Janneke lends a hand. She lifts up the bike. And Jip scrambles to his feet. He's got a big graze on his cheek. And another one on his knee.

Here comes Father back out of the house. 'What's this?' he says. 'Jip, you were only supposed to put the bike away.'

'I know,' says Jip. 'But I can ride it too.' And he smiles through his tears.

And then Janneke goes into the house with Jip. And she helps Jip wash his face.

'Those kids,' Father says. 'They're already riding bikes.'

Amsterdam Zoo

'Where shall we go first?' Aunty Trudy asks. 'The monkeys? Or the tigers?'

'The monkeys,' says Jip.

'Yes, the monkeys,' says Janneke.

They've got a big bag of nuts. For the monkeys. Look, there are the rocks where the monkeys live.

'Here, monkey!' Jip calls. 'Have a nut.' And he holds one out.

'Throw it to him,' says Aunty Trudy.

Jip throws it. And the monkey picks it up. Janneke roars with laughter. The monkeys are going crazy. They're jumping around all over the place. And there's a mother monkey. With a baby monkey. And the mother monkey jumps up really high. And she doesn't even hold on to the baby.

'Oh no, that baby's going to fall...' says Janneke.

'No, it won't,' says Aunty Trudy. 'It's holding on really tight. See.'

Now they walk on. Look, there's a camel. With children on its back.

'Would you like to go on the camel too?' asks Aunty Trudy.

'Yes, please,' Jip shouts. 'I want to go on the camel.'

'Me too,' says Janneke.

But she's a little bit scared.

'All right,' says Aunty Trudy. 'Come on.'

The camel is really big. 'It's too high up,' says Jip. But then the camel lowers itself down. It goes down on its knees. Then it folds its legs up completely. And now Jip can climb up onto it. And so can Janneke. They're sitting there. Between the two humps.

'You all right there?' the keeper asks.

Yes, they're fine. It's nice and soft. But Janneke is a bit worried. Now the camel stands up. Whoa, it's really high up. Jip holds on tight to a tuft of hair. And Janneke holds on with both hands too. Fortunately the camel has tufts of hair sticking out all over the place. It's a very messy animal. It needs a good brush.

Off they go. It walks very slowly. But it lurches like anything. Whoops, to the left. And whoops, to the right. Just like a boat. 'Is it nice up there?' Aunty Trudy calls. She's so far away now.

They're so high up.

'It's great!' Jip calls back. He lets go with one hand and waves.

The camel walks around in a circle. And then it stops. It kneels again.

'So,' says the keeper. 'Off you get.' He lifts Jip down first. And then Janneke.

Janneke is blushing.

'I did it,' she says.

'You were very brave,' says Aunty Trudy.

'It was smelly,' says Jip. 'That camel stinks. It needs a bath. And its hair is really dirty.'

'Camels never have baths,' says Aunty Trudy. 'They don't need them.'

'And now I want to go on the elephant!' Jip shouts.

But no, you're not allowed to go for a ride on the elephant. You're only allowed to look at it.

And then they go to see the lion. There is so much to see at Amsterdam zoo.

But the camel is still the best.

Much Too Cold

Jip and Janneke are going out. For a drive.

It's Sunday. And Uncle Hank says, 'Where shall we go?'

'Schiphol,' says Jip. 'I want to see the planes.'

'No,' says Janneke. 'The seaside. I want to go to the beach.'

'We'll draw straws,' says Uncle Hank. 'Here, I've got two sticks in my hand. See? I'm holding them tight and you can't tell which one is longer, can you?'

'No,' says Jip.

'No,' says Janneke. 'They're the same.'

'That's what you think,' says Uncle Hank. 'Now you both pull a stick out of my hand. And the one who gets the longest stick wins.'

'Me first,' says Jip.

'No,' says Uncle Hank. 'Ladies first. Janneke gets to choose.'

Janneke pulls a stick out of Uncle Hank's hand.

And Jip pulls out the other stick.

'Mine's longer,' says Janneke.

She's right. Janneke's stick is longer.

'You win,' says Uncle Hank. 'We're going to the seaside.'

'Yippee!' screams Janneke.

And now Jip thinks it's fun too. 'I'm going to go for a paddle,' he says.

'No, you're not,' says Uncle Hank. 'It's much too cold for that.'

Off they go. Jip and Janneke are allowed to sit in the front. Next to Uncle Hank. But Jip isn't allowed to touch anything. That would be dangerous. He's not allowed to pull on any of the knobs. Or hold onto the steering wheel.

But they still pretend they're steering. Both of them. And they make engine noises, just like a real car: Brrrm-brm.

'There's the sea,' says Uncle Hank. 'We'll park the car here. And then we'll go for a walk.'

It is a little cold. And it's windy. But it's still lovely.

'Look at those waves!' shouts Jip. And he walks up really close to the water in his wellies. Whoosh! Here comes a wave. Jip jumps back.

Janneke does it too. But she isn't wearing wellies. She's got shoes on. Whoosh! Here comes a wave. Janneke tries to run away. But it's too late. Her feet are sopping wet.

Oh, oh, it's so cold.

'Now I'm going to take off my shoes,' says Janneke. 'And my socks too.'

And there goes Janneke, running around barefoot.

But Uncle Hank doesn't want her to. 'You'll catch a cold,' he says. 'Come on, we're going back home.'

'I've found a shell,' Jip shouts. 'A big beautiful shell! And another one! This one's for you, Janneke.'

And then they get back in the car. Janneke with bare feet. And with a shell each.

'There,' says Uncle Hank when they're back home. 'When it's summer, I'll come and pick you up again. Then you can go for a proper swim. Bye!'

'Bye,' shout Jip and Janneke.

Peacock

Jip and Janneke have to go to the farm. To get some eggs.

'What's that?' cries Jip. 'Look over there.'

'A turkey!' screams Janneke.

No, two! Two big fat turkeys are coming towards them.

They're making funny noises. They say, 'Gobble, gobble.'

'Move over,' Jip shouts. 'You're in the way.'

But the turkeys don't care.

Here comes the farmer.

'Ah, look who's here,' she says. 'How many eggs would you like today?'

'A dozen,' says Janneke. 'Fresh ones.'

'I'll make sure they're very fresh,' says the farmer. 'Would you like to see the calves too?'

Jip and Janneke go to see the calves. They're really sweet.

'And look, there's the peacock,' says the farmer.

They've never seen a peacock before. It has a long tail that drags over the ground. It makes a rustling noise with its tail. And then all at once it shrieks.

'Why's it making that horrible noise?' asks Jip.

'Look,' says Janneke, 'look.'

The peacock is putting up its tail. It's amazing. It stands very still. And it looks very proud. With its tail feathers spread out in a big circle behind it. And a little crown on its head.

Jip and Janneke stay there for a long time looking at the peacock. They think it's really beautiful.

And then the peacock puts its tail down again. 'So, the show's over,' says the farmer. 'Off you go. With your eggs.'

Jip and Janneke go back home. And they hear the peacock shriek again. What a horrible noise.

'I want a peacock,' Jip tells his mother. 'Like the peacock at the farm.'

'Goodness,' says Mother. 'A peacock. Whatever for?'

'It's got such a beautiful tail,' says Jip.

'But they make a really horrible noise,' says Janneke. 'I don't want any peacocks.'

'We'll look for a peacock that can sing,' says Father. 'And if we find one, we'll buy it.'

'We're going back to the farm again tomorrow,' says Janneke. 'There are so many fun animals there.'

Bouncy

There are two sheep in the meadow. They've got lambs. Two little lambs each. Jip and Janneke go to have a look.

'That one's the cutest,' says Janneke.

'Yes,' Jip says, 'it jumps so high. And it's got such beautiful curls!'

The farmer comes out. 'Hello,' he says. 'How do you like the lambs?'

'They're lovely,' says Jip, 'and that one's the nicest.'

'Okay,' says the farmer. 'That can be your lamb. Why don't you give it a name? And then you can play with it.'

The farmer goes away. And Janneke says, 'What shall we call it?'

'Pete,' says Jip.

'No,' Janneke says. 'Pete isn't a name for a lamb. We'll call it Bouncy. Because it's just like a bouncy ball of wool.'

'Let's take it home with us,' says Jip.

'Is that allowed?'

'Of course. It's our lamb, isn't it? The farmer said so.'

And together Jip and Janneke pick up the little lamb. It kicks and wriggles. And it calls out, 'Maaaaa!'

'Come on,' says Jip. 'We'll take you to my mother.' And they take the little lamb home with them.

'What have you got there?' asks Jip's mother.

'This is Bouncy,' Jip says. 'It's ours. The farmer said so.'

'But we can't keep a sheep here,' Mother says. 'What are we supposed to do with it?'

'Oh, please,' Jip and Janneke beg.

'Now listen,' Mother says. 'That lamb wants to go back to its mother. What would you say, Jip, if a big boy came along and carried you off? And took you to his house? That wouldn't be right, would it? And that lamb's mother is very worried.'

'But it's ours,' Janneke says.

'Yes,' says Mother, 'it's yours. Here's a blue ribbon. Tie it round its neck. And then put it back with its mother. Then the lamb will be happy again. And you'll still know which lamb is yours.'

So the lamb goes back to the meadow. And it gets to wear a blue ribbon.

'Bye-bye, Bouncy,' says Jip.

'Bye, Bouncy,' says Janneke. 'We'll come back tomorrow.'

'Maaaa,' says Bouncy.

Rowing Boat

On the other side of the meadow there's a canal. And in that canal there's a rowing boat.

There is a man in the rowing boat. It's Mr Bakker from up the street. Jip and Janneke are watching him.

'Would you like to come for a ride?' he asks.

'Yes, please,' say Jip and Janneke.

'Come on then,' he says.

He lifts Jip into the boat. And then he lifts Janneke into the boat. He puts them down next to each other on a little bench.

'Off we go,' says Mr Bakker. And he grabs the oars and starts to row.

Off they go. It's wonderful. They go really fast.

The water splashes around the boat. And they row past reeds. And past flowers. Jip and Janneke really like it.

'I'm going to stop here,' says Mr Bakker. 'You'll have to wait for a moment.'

He ties the boat up next to a farmhouse. And he gets out. And now Jip and Janneke are sitting in the boat. Alone.

'Shall I do some rowing?' Jip asks.

'No, don't,' Janneke says. 'It's not allowed. The boat will drift off. And then we'll sink.

'No, we won't,' says Jip. 'I can do it.'

But here's Mr Bakker again. He says, 'So, kids, off we go again. Would you like to do some rowing?'

'Yes, please,' says Jip.

And Mr Bakker lets Jip sit next to him on his bench. And he gives him the two big oars to hold.

But, oof, they're so heavy. They are so heavy. Jip can't row. He's too little.

'I can't do it...' Jip says.

'Wait until you're big,' says Mr Bakker. 'And now let me take over again.'

And then they row back.

It's a lovely trip.

On the Ferry

Mother is in the middle. And Jip is walking on one side and Janneke is walking on the other side.

'And now we're going on the ferry,' says Mother. They're on their way to see Aunty Molly. She lives on the other side of the river. It's a long way away. First they went on the bus. For a whole hour. And now they're going on the ferry.

'What's a ferry?' Janneke asks.

'It's a boat,' says Mother. 'A big, flat boat. And all the cars go on it. And all the bikes. And all the people too.'

'Oh, look,' Jip shouts, 'I can already see the water. Is that the ferry?'

'That's it. See? It's already got cars on it. And a horse and cart. And loads of bikes!'

Jip does a little jig. He thinks it's wonderful.

'Not so fast,' says Mother. 'Stay with me. It's so busy! Come on, now it's time for us to go on too.'

Jip is already running ahead.

But Janneke doesn't want to go. She pulls on Mother's arm. She freezes. On the bank.

'What's all this?' Mother asks. 'Why don't you want to go on the ferry?'

At first Janneke doesn't want to say anything. She looks very scared.

And she's crying a little bit.

'Is it too busy for you?' Mother asks. 'It's not that bad.'

But Janneke says, 'Is it going to start sailing, the boat?'

'Yes, of course, it will sail in a minute.'

And then Janneke sobs. 'It's already got so many cars on it. If I go on too, the boat will sink!'

That makes Mother laugh. 'No, it won't,' she says. 'Don't worry.'

'Come on,' Jip calls. 'If it sinks, I'll rescue you.'

And then Janneke's brave enough.

Look, they're standing on the ferry. And they make it safely to the other side.

Lots and Lots of Ice Creams

The ice-cream man is standing on the corner of the street.

Jip heard him coming ages ago. He drags Janneke straight to his mother.

'May we have an ice cream, please, Mother?'

'All right, then,' says Mother.

She gives Jip and Janneke some money. For a large ice cream each.

'Nice, huh?' says Janneke. 'I dare you to bite it.'

Jip's not scared to bite it. In three bites his ice cream is gone.

Janneke takes a little longer. It's so cold!

Just when they've finished their ice creams, Jip's father comes by. On his bike. He looks at Jip and Janneke first, and then at the ice-cream man.

'Would you like an ice cream?' he asks.

'Yes, please,' say Jip and Janneke. And Father buys them ice creams.

'Bye,' he says. 'I hope they taste good.'

And again their ice creams are finished in no time.

'Let's go to my house now,' says Janneke. And Jip goes to her house with her.

'Mother,' Janneke calls. 'The ice-cream man is here.'

'Oh,' says Janneke's mother. 'Is it that time of year already? Here's some money. For a small ice cream each.'

Jip and Janneke run back to the cart. 'So,' says the ice-cream man, 'you two can put them away!' And, yes, soon they've finished these ones too.

And here comes Janneke's father. On his bike.

'Hello,' he calls. 'Would you like an ice cream?'

'Yes, please,' say Jip and Janneke very sweetly.

Janneke's father buys two more large ones.

But when they're back at Jip's a little later, they're very quiet. They're sitting on the sofa. Not moving and not saying a word.

'How many ice creams have you had?' Mother asks.

'Four,' says Jip. He looks a little pale.

'Four?' says Mother. 'In fifteen minutes? That's terrible! Now you've both turned your stomachs into ice-cream slides. Now you won't be able to eat any potatoes.'

'Why not?' Jip asks.

'Because the potatoes will slide down,' says Mother. 'They'll slide down really fast. That's what you get.'

But Jip and Janneke don't want to eat any potatoes. They don't want to eat anything ever again. Never ever.

The Sun Did It

'Don't stay in the water too long, Jip! Come out of the water, Jip!' But Jip thinks it's so lovely in the sea. He doesn't want to come out. And Mother has been standing there calling for so long, 'Come out now, Jip.' It's such beautiful weather. And the sun is shining. And the sea is so blue. And they're going to stay at the beach all day, all day! That's why Jip doesn't want to come back out of the water ever again. Janneke got out ages ago. She's already having a nap in the shade. She was so tired from the waves.

Now Mother's getting impatient.

'I'll come in and get you,' she shouts.

'Yoo-hoo,' screams Jip. And he runs away as fast as he can, going further into the sea.

He goes so deep, so deep.

And here comes Mother. She grabs Jip by his bathing trunks and pulls him out of the water.

Jip bellows. Jip is furious.

But Mother dries him off with a towel. And Mother plonks him down in the shade next to Janneke. 'Shhh,' she says. 'Janneke's asleep. You go to sleep too, Jip.'

It doesn't take long. In no time Jip's sleeping like a baby.

But when he wakes up! Ow, it hurts. His back hurts. His arm hurts so much. And he's turned bright red.

'Serves you right,' says Mother. 'Now you're sunburnt.'

'I can't be,' Jip says. 'I was in the water.'

'Yes,' says Mother, 'but the sun can still burn you. I'll put something on it. There, that will help.'

'Ow,' Jip screams.

And on the way home on the train, Jip can't stop crying. 'It hurts so much,' he says. 'It really, really hurts.'

'Shall I blow on it for you?' Janneke asks. 'Then it won't hurt anymore.' And she blows on Jip's neck. And over his back. And into his shirt.

'See,' says Janneke, 'now it's better.'

But it isn't really and it takes a whole day to stop hurting.

'I'm never going to stay in the sea that long again,' says Jip.

Radishes

'Do you want to come to my house for lunch?' asks Janneke. 'We've got strawberries.'

'Can I?' Jip asks.

'Of course,' says Mother. 'Go and have lunch at Janneke's.'

Jip goes off with Janneke. He always loves it when he gets to eat at Janneke's. He always eats a lot more.

Look, there's a big bowl full of strawberries. They're such a beautiful red.

'Squash them on a slice of bread,' says Janneke's mother. 'And then, sprinkle some sugar on top. Castor sugar. Yum.'

Jip eats five slices. And Janneke eats four. And now they've got fat little tummies. They can't even play tag anymore. They can't run.

'Are you coming to my house tomorrow?' Jip asks. 'Do you want to come and eat strawberries at my house?'

But, oh, the next day, Jip has a rash. With lots of little bumps. And it's so itchy.

'Don't scratch like that, Jip,' says Mother. 'You'll scratch them open.'

But the itch makes Jip really angry. He pulls a horrible face. And he can't stop scratching.

'It's from the strawberries,' Mother says. 'You're not allowed to eat them anymore. They give you a rash.'

Oh, how horrible. Janneke's coming for lunch. And now they won't get any strawberries.

'You can have radishes,' says Mother. 'They're red too. And delicious. And they won't give you a rash.'

Jip and Janneke eat lots of sandwiches. With radishes. And they have one big radish – that's the mother. And another big one is the father. And six little ones are the children.

They get to go in Jip's truck. It's fun. The whole radish family goes for a drive. But when they've done enough driving around, things go badly for them.

Jip and Janneke eat them up. The whole radish family gets eaten up. Sad, isn't it?

Scooters

Janneke's sitting on the floor. And she's not doing anything. She's just sitting there.

And Janneke's mother says, 'Don't you want to go to Jip's?'

'No,' says Janneke.

'Shouldn't you be outside playing with Jip?'

'No,' says Janneke.

And Janneke looks really sad.

'Did you two have a fight?' Mother asks.

'No,' says Janneke. 'We didn't have a fight.'

'What's wrong then?'

'Jip's got a scooter,' says Janneke.

Mother looks out. And there's Jip out in the street. Whizzing by on his scooter. He's going really fast. Really, really fast. And he shoots around the corner on his scooter. And he doesn't have time to play with Janneke. It's like he's forgotten all about Janneke.

And that's why Janneke's so sad. She's

just sitting on the floor and doesn't want to do anything.

'Jip will be back here soon enough,' says Mother. 'He'll get sick of that scooter.'

But he doesn't. Jip rides around on the scooter all day every day.

And then Janneke's mother says, 'This has gone on long enough. You're getting a scooter too. But you have to promise to stay on the pavement, Janneke!'

And Janneke promises.

Janneke gets a really beautiful scooter. And now they're together again. They go all the way to the end of the street. And Janneke's mother stands at the window and watches.

'Beep! Beep!' screams Jip, swerving past on his scooter.

'Bang! Bang!' shouts Janneke, trying to keep up with him. Because Jip can still go a lot faster than she can.

Stinging Nettles

Close to home there's a path. And if you follow that path, you come to a small dike. A dike you can roll down.

It's not always allowed. Because the dike is dirty.

But today Jip's mother says, 'If you put on your old trousers and your old т-shirt, it's all right.'

Jip goes to get Janneke.

'Wait a minute,' she says. 'I'm going to put on some trousers.' And she runs inside. A little later she comes back out. And now she's wearing old clothes too. And together they go rolling down the dike. It's great fun. If you start all the way up at the top, you go faster and faster.

'I'll race you to the bottom,' says Jip.

'Okay,' says Janneke.

They both lie down on top of the dike.

'One, two, three, go!' says Jip. And they're off. They're picking up speed. Oh, they're going so fast!

Jip is much further down than Janneke. Jip's going to win! But wait, now Janneke's going a lot faster. Janneke rolls past Jip.

They're at the bottom. But Jip's rolled into a puddle! And Janneke's ended up in a clump of stinging nettles.

Jip's crying, 'Oh, Janneke, look at me. I'm all covered in mud!'

But Janneke isn't listening to Jip. She's yelling at the top of her voice. Because the nettles have stung her. They've stung her a lot. And she's covered with little red lumps. Her hands are covered with little red lumps and so is her face. Jip forgets about the mud. And he takes Janneke by the hand.

'Come on,' he says. 'Mother's got something to put on it.'

Soon they're back at Jip's.

'What happened?' asks Mother. 'Jip, look at you! You look like a pig. And why is Janneke crying?'

'Janneke rolled into the stinging nettles,' says Jip.

'Oh, you poor thing. Come with me,'

says Mother. 'I'll put some cream on it. Then it will be better in no time.'

Mother takes Janneke to the bathroom, because that's where they keep the first-aid kit.

'From now on you'd better not roll down that dike anymore,' says Mother. 'You either get dirty or you end up in the nettles.'

Making Pancakes

'Is that a real stove?' asks Jip

'Uh-huh,' says Janneke. 'It's all real.'

'Is not,' says Jip. 'I don't believe a word of it.' He sticks out a hand and touches the stove.

'Ow,' he yelps.

'See,' says Janneke. 'I told you it was real.'

It's hot! It burns.

Jip puts his finger in his mouth. It hurts. But now he believes her.

'Look,' says Janneke. 'Sit down there. Then I'll make you some pancakes.'

'Okay,' says Jip. 'I'll be the daddy. And you can be the mummy.'

He sits down at the table. And he waits.

Janneke makes a pancake. She has a very small frying pan. And she has a mixing bowl full of batter. And a small wooden spoon. It smells delicious already.

But now she has to flip the pancake.

'Wait,' she says. 'I can do it. Mother taught me. I'll throw it up in the air. And then I'll catch it again.'

Whoosh! Janneke throws the pancake up into the air.

But, oh, she doesn't catch it. It falls on the floor.

'Snap,' goes Weenie.

'Hey!' yells Janneke.

'No!' screams Jip.

That naughty dog. He's eaten the whole pancake!

'You chase him off, Jip,' says Janneke. 'Then I'll make a new one.'

And the second pancake? That turns out. It's a beautiful yellow. And it tastes delicious.

Janneke makes six. Three each. And then the batter's finished.

And Weenie doesn't get any more at all.

On the Merry-go-round

'There's a merry-go-round,' cries Jip. 'A real merry-go-round. With horses!'

Jip and Janneke go to have a look. It's not a real fun fair. Just a little one. There's a merry-go-round. And swinging chairs.

The swinging chairs are high up and scary. But the merry-go-round is beautiful. There are horses that go round in circles. A green one and a yellow one and a pink one. And look, there's a swan you can sit on too. And a bear and an elephant.

'Mother, it costs money!' Jip calls out. And Janneke goes home too and asks, 'Mother, may I have some money for the merry-go-round, please?'

They both get enough money for two goes. And Jip sits on the bear. And Janneke sits on a horse. And then a bell rings. Ting-a-ling, ting-a-ling... And off it goes... really fast. Around and around and around and around. It's wonderful. Jip looks back and sees Janneke behind him on the horse.

'Hi!' he calls. And he waves with one hand.

'Hi!' Janneke calls back. But she holds on tight with both hands. She's a little scared.

Oh, now it's slowing down. Now it's hardly moving at all. Now it's stopped!

'Again,' says Janneke. 'We can have another turn.'

They go on it again. But it's finished so soon.

'Come on,' says Jip. 'Let's go home and ask again.'

But Jip's mother says, 'You can't keep going on it forever.' And Janneke's mother says, 'You can go again tomorrow.'

Jip and Janneke are sad. But they go back to watch the merry-go-round anyway.

And at half past twelve Jip's father comes past. On his bike.

'Do you want to have a go?' he asks, getting off his bike. Jip and Janneke get some more money from Jip's father. And then some more again after that.

Then Father gives them a ride home on his bike. For lunch.

'We went on it four times!' shouts Jip.

'Oh,' says Mother. 'You two are so spoilt!'

What a Naughty Little Girl

Jip and Janneke have to go to the green-grocer's. They have to buy some apples. Star apples. They're the red ones. They shine up really well.

The greengrocer gives them boiled sweets. And then they go to the baker's. They get a boiled sweet each there too. And then they go to the grocery. There they get liquorice.

'Have you got the apples?' Mother asks when they get home.

'Yes,' says Jip. 'Here they are. And we went to the baker's too.'

'And we went to the grocery,' says Janneke.

'You didn't need to go there, did you?' says Mother. 'What did you buy?'

'Nothing,' says Jip. 'We just went into the shop. And they gave us some boiled sweets.'

'That's right,' Janneke says. 'And the grocer gave us some liquorice. We only went into the shop there too. And we said, "We don't have to buy anything here."'

'You mustn't do that,' says Mother.

'I'm going to go and change Dolly-Dee,' says Janneke. 'She has to go to bed.'

But where is Dolly-Dee? She's gone.

'We took her with us,' says Jip. 'We took her with us when we went to do the shopping.'

Oh no, now Dolly-Dee is missing.

'Go back to the greengrocer's,' says Mother. 'Maybe she's still there.'

But there's no Dolly-Dee at the green-grocer's.

'The baker's then,' says Jip.

They go back to the bakery. But the baker says, 'No, sorry, you didn't leave any dolls here.'

Then they go to the grocery.

'Did you see a doll here?' asks Jip.

'No,' says the grocer. 'I didn't see anything.'

A very sad Jip and a very sad Janneke start to leave. But just when they are about to step through the door, Janneke sees Dolly-Dee. She's sitting on a sack of nuts.

'There she is!' cries Janneke. And she grabs Dolly-Dee. 'Naughty little girl,' she says. 'Wandering off like that.'

And then they go home.

'We found her,' calls Jip.

'Lovely,' says Mother. 'Had you left her at the greengrocer's?'

'No,' says Janneke. 'At the grocery. And she was sitting on a sack of nuts. And I really didn't put her there. She walked off by herself.'

'I don't believe that,' says Mother.

Walking through a Big Puddle

It's raining! It's raining! It's pouring down. And there are big puddles in the street. And water is gushing out of the drainpipes. Everyone is staying inside. Except Jip. Because Jip has a set of waterproofs. And Jip has wellies. It doesn't bother Jip. First he steps over the puddles. Then he walks through them carefully. Then he goes and stands in the middle of a puddle. And he stamps very hard, so that the water splashes up around his ears.

And Janneke? Janneke is sitting by the window. She doesn't have a set of waterproofs. And she doesn't have any wellies. And that's why she's not allowed to go outside. She is very jealous of Jip. Poor Janneke. She watches and she watches. And Jip puts on a show for her. He takes a big run up and jumps right into the middle of the puddle. What a splash!

'Mother,' Janneke asks, 'can't I, just for a little while?'

'You'll get your feet wet,' says Mother. 'You don't have any wellies.'

Then Janneke's father comes in. He says, 'I've got an idea. You can wear my boots. And then you can go out for a little while with Jip.'

Janneke puts on Father's boots. They're enormous! She can hardly walk. But she goes out anyway and stands next to Jip in the puddle and says, 'Look.'

'Hey,' Jip shouts, 'you look just like Tom Thumb.'

Janneke tries to walk really fast. Like Tom Thumb.

But, oh! Oh no! She's fallen over!

Face first in the puddle.

And now Janneke is filthy. She's covered in mud.

'Jip, inside now,' Jip's mother calls.

'Janneke, inside now,' Janneke's father calls.

The fun is over. Janneke has to have a bath.

'It was just for a little while,' Janneke says, 'but it was still lovely.'

The King and the Queen

It's raining. Jip and Janneke can't go outside. They have to play inside. And they're very grumpy. They're not in a good mood at all. Finally Mother says, 'I know. Today you can play with the chest.'

And that's wonderful. Because there are all kinds of things inside that chest. All kinds of clothes. Now they can dress up. They can act out a story.

'Look,' says Janneke. 'There's a gold crown. And another one.'

She's right, there are two gold crowns in the chest. Made of paper. They look just like real crowns. 'I'm the queen,' says Janneke. 'And you can be the king.'

Janneke puts a curtain on her head. And then she puts the crown on over it.

And Jip finds a fur cape. Mother's old fur. It's beautiful. It is a bit moth-eaten. But that doesn't matter. Now he's a real king. He puts a crown on too.

They stroll across the room.

'Ready for dinner, dear?' Janneke asks.

'Don't talk like that,' Jip says. 'A queen doesn't talk like that. A queen says, "Would you care to eat now, Your Majesty?"'

'She does not,' says Janneke. 'I'm not going to talk to my own husband like that. A queen doesn't call her own husband Your Majesty.'

'Yes, she does!' shouts Jip.

'Doesn't!' shouts Janneke.

'You're not playing anymore!' screams Jip. And he pulls off Janneke's crown. But Janneke gets very angry. She hits him and she kicks him.

Oh no, what a terrible king. And what a terrible queen. Now they're fighting.

The king's crown is all dented. And hanging down around his nose.

And the queen's train is torn.

When Mother comes in, she's very sad. 'I thought you were playing so nicely together,' she says. 'And now you're fighting. Take those clothes off right away. Everything back in the chest.'

Jip and Janneke tidy up. They're a little bit embarrassed.

'Look,' says Mother, 'there's the sun! Hurry on out, Your Majesties.'

And Jip and Janneke run outside.

Lost

'Look,' Jip says. 'There's Saint Nicholas.'

'Where?' asks Janneke.

'There!' Jip shouts. And he points. And he's right, Saint Nicholas is there. A long way down the street. He's walking along the pavement with his helper, Pete. But they don't have the horse with them.

'Look at all those kids,' says Jip.

'Let's go see,' says Janneke.

And off go Jip and Janneke. They run. They run really fast. Because they can see Saint Nicholas in the distance. With lots of children following him.

'We're catching up,' says Jip.

He's panting.

'We are,' says Janneke.

And they run and they run. But Jip has short little legs. And so does Janneke.

They can't run that fast yet.

'They went down this street,' says Jip.

'No, they didn't,' says Janneke. 'The next one.'

Then Jip and Janneke go down a side street. And it's crowded with people. People looking at the shop windows.

But Saint Nicholas has disappeared.

'We'll go down this street,' says Jip. 'They must be here.' And they go down yet another street.

But Saint Nicholas isn't there either.

'Now I don't know anymore,' Janneke says. 'Where are we now?'

'I don't know,' says Jip.

They don't know where they are anymore. They're lost. And Saint Nicholas is nowhere to be seen. Jip starts to cry. And Janneke starts to cry too. They go and stand in the middle of the street. They are really howling.

'Hey, Jip, what are you doing here?' asks a voice.

Jip looks up.

It's one of their neighbours. It's Mr Bakker.

'We don't know where we live anymore,' says Jip. And the tears are rolling down his cheeks.

'We're lost,' says Janneke.

'Come with me,' says Mr Bakker. 'I can drive you home in my car. I'll take you home.'

He picks up Jip. And he picks up Janneke. And he puts them both in the car.

It's wonderful.

'What were you doing so far from home?' asks Mr Bakker.

'We saw Saint Nicholas,' says Jip. 'And we wanted to follow him. And then he disappeared.'

'Oh,' says Mr Bakker. 'Saint Nicholas is going to come to your house too, isn't he?'

'Do you think so?' asks Jip.

'I'm sure of it,' says Mr Bakker. 'Now

run off home. And tonight you can put out your shoe.'

Jip's mother is standing in front of her door. And Janneke's mother is standing in front of her door too.

'Where were you?' they ask anxiously. 'Did you run away?'

Jip and Janneke tell them the whole story.

'But we got a nice ride in Mr Bakker's car,' they say. 'It was fun!'

'Well,' says Jip's mother. 'Maybe Saint Nicholas will still come to our house.'

'Or our house, huh, Mother?' Janneke asks.

'Or our house,' says Janneke's mother.

Singing for Saint Nicholas

Jip and Janneke are standing in front of the fireplace. They have to sing a song. A song for Saint Nicholas.

'Nicholas, you rascal, you,' Jip sings at the top of his voice, 'Put a present in my shoe.'

'Hark, who's knocking, children!' shouts Janneke, even louder.

'Listen,' Father says, 'you can't do it like that. If you sing songs, you have to do it together. You have to sing the same song. Otherwise it sounds horrible.'

But Jip only wants to do 'Nicholas, You Rascal, You'.

And Janneke only wants to do 'Hark, Who's Knocking, Children'.

And they start fighting.

And Jip kicks the shoe Janneke has put out for Saint Nicholas.

And Janneke picks up Jip's shoe and throws it through the room. And the hay they've left there for the horse goes flying.

'Have you gone completely mad?' snaps Mother. 'This is a nice way to behave. If Saint Nicholas is watching he'll be very sad.'

'Is he on the roof now?' Jip asks.

'Probably,' says Father.

'I'll go have a look,' says Jip. And he tries to go out on the street.

'No!' Father shouts. And he manages to grab Jip by his pyjama jacket just in time. 'What are you thinking? It's cold and dark out there!'

'Come on,' says Mother. 'I'll sing with you. First we'll do "Nicholas, You Rascal, You". And then "Hark, Who's Knocking, Children".'

And now it goes well.

Jip gives Janneke a kiss.

And Janneke gives Jip a kiss.

And together they tidy up the hay.

And then they go to bed.

Bad Seagulls

In Jip's garden there's a birdhouse. When it's cold, birds go there to eat. There are bits of bread inside it. And there's a string of monkey nuts and an old sunflower. The birds pick the seeds out of it.

'Can we feed the birds too?' Janneke asks. And they're allowed to. Father gives them a big chunk of stale bread each. And they break it into pieces and spread it out in the garden, just near the back door. First some sparrows come. And then a blackbird.

But then they hear loud screeching. There are seagulls in the sky. Big white seagulls. They come closer and closer. They chase off the sparrows. And they chase off the blackbird. And then they chase the little tits away too. And then they eat all the bread.

'That's mean!' Janneke shouts.

'Yeah,' says Jip. 'It's cheating. Go away, seagulls.' And he waves his arms furiously at the seagulls, who are so greedy. The seagulls fly off. They're scared of Jip.

'Come back now, sparrows,' Janneke calls. 'Come back, tits! They're gone now.'

But the sparrows don't come back. And neither do the tits. And the blackbird doesn't come back either.

'Look what you've done,' Mother says. 'Silly Jip. You've chased all the birds away. Come inside now. Then they'll come back.'

And thank goodness, once Jip and Janneke are inside again and sitting on the window-seat, the sparrows come back. And they fill their tummies.

Frost

Jip wakes up. And he looks out through the window. Oh, wow, everything's white. 'Snow!' shouts Jip.

'No,' says Mother. 'It's not snow. It's freezing outside. The grass is white from the frost.'

'I want to go outside,' Jip says.

'Breakfast first,' says Mother.

Jip eats his breakfast. And here comes Janneke. She's wearing a woolly hat. And woollen mittens. And a thick scarf. And trousers.

'You coming, Jip?' Janneke asks. 'Everything's frozen.'

And Jip dresses up warm too. And Jip goes outside with Janneke. It is so beautiful. Everything's white.

The branches of the trees are white. And so is the grass. And the hedge. And the fence. You can write on it with your finger. Now they're at the ditch. It's covered with ice. But the ice is still very thin.

'Are you brave enough to walk on it?' Janneke asks.

'No,' says Jip. 'It's dangerous. It's not allowed either.'

'Would you fall through it?' Janneke asks.

'I think so,' says Jip.

'Is Weenie brave enough? He's so little. He won't fall through it.'

'Go on the ice, Weenie,' says Jip.

But Weenie's too scared. He stays on the side.

'Go on,' shouts Janneke, throwing a stone onto the ice.

But Weenie won't fetch the stone. He's scared. He doesn't want to go on the ice.

'Here, Weenie,' says Jip. 'Bring back this big stone.' And he throws a big stone onto the ice.

Crack, says the ice. And it's broken. There's a beautiful star in it. See, it is too early to go on the ice.

Jip and Janneke go back inside. Because it's windy. And it's really cold. Weenie's shivering. But that's because Weenie doesn't have a woolly hat on. Or a scarf. Or trousers.

New Year's Eve

It's dark outside. And really cold. And it's the middle of the night. Jip is in bed. He's asleep.

But then suddenly: Boom, boom, toot, toot! Boom! What is that? Jip wakes up. He sits up in bed. And he gets really scared. Because there's such a racket. It sounds like guns. And he hears a ship in the distance. And another one. And he hears yelling out on the street. What's going on? And then suddenly Jip remembers. It's New Year's Eve! Father and Mother are downstairs. With Aunty Trudy. They're celebrating the New Year. He can hear them laughing.

Jip gets out of bed. And tiptoes down the stairs. He walks into the hall. And then he opens the door very quietly. The door to the living room. Look, there's Father. Holding a glass. And Mother too. And Aunty Trudy as well. They don't see Jip. Jip goes into the room.

And then Father sees him. He says, 'Look who we have here. What are you doing up, you little rascal?'

And Mother gives him a kiss. And she

says, 'Happy New Year, Jip.'

'I want a glass of something too,' says Jip.

'You can have an apple fritter,' says Aunty Trudy. 'Come and sit on my lap.'

Jip is very sleepy. But it's so nice to be there. He eats his apple fritter. With tiny little bites.

'Now I'm going to play with my car,' Jip says.

But Father says, 'No, Jip, that's enough now. I'm taking you back to bed.'

Jip falls asleep again right away. And the next morning Janneke comes to visit.

'Happy New Year,' she says.

'Happy New Year,' says Jip. 'I stayed up last night.'

'No, you didn't,' says Janneke.

'Yes, I did,' Jip says. 'I was allowed to stay up until twelve o'clock.'

'You're fibbing,' says Janneke.

'I'm not fibbing,' says Jip.

But Mother says, 'Jip went to bed at seven o'clock. Like always. But he came downstairs at twelve o'clock. Just for a moment. Didn't you, Jip?'

'That's right,' says Jip. 'And I had an apple fritter. And I heard the fireworks.'

And Janneke is jealous. Because she was asleep all night. And she didn't hear any fireworks. 'I think it's mean,' she says. 'I want to hear the fireworks too.'

But Jip's mother says, 'I saved an apple fritter for you, Janneke. And don't be sad. You'll hear more than enough fireworks when you're big.'

Bye, Jip! Bye, Janneke!

'Aren't you ready yet?' Jip calls. 'You have to hurry up! Come on!'

'There's still plenty of time,' says Mother. 'The bus doesn't leave for a half hour yet.'

But Jip is so scared they'll be late. He shouts at Janneke, 'Hurry up! Hurry up!'

Jip and Janneke are going to stay at Aunty Trudy's. Together. For a really long time. Look, there's Jip's case. It's got lots of things in it. Clothes. And a toothbrush. And a pair of pyjamas. And another pair. And a dressing gown. And three cars. And a little tow truck. And here comes Janneke. She's got a case too. And what's in it? Dolly-Dee. She's on top of everything else. She has to spend a long time inside the case.

But she doesn't mind. She's not scared of the dark. What else is in the case? There's a pair of pyjamas. And another pair. And a dressing gown. And a real dress. With lace. And other clothes too. And a bag of sweets. And a present for Aunty Trudy.

'So,' says Jip's mother. 'Time to go.'

Because Jip's mother is going to see Jip and Janneke off.

'Put your raincoat on, Jip. And you too, Janneke. You'll be sure to need it.'

'Will you be good at Aunty Trudy's?'

'Yes,' say Jip and Janneke.

'And you won't fight?'

'No,' says Jip.

'No,' says Janneke.

'My case is a lot nicer than yours,' says Jip.

'No, it's not. Mine's nicer,' says Janneke.

'Your case is dirty,' says Jip. And he kicks it.

That makes Janneke cross. She kicks back at Jip. She kicks him in the leg.

'Listen,' says Mother. 'That's no way to start. Come on, we're going back home. We're not going to the bus. Children who pick fights with each other can't go away to stay at someone else's house.'

'We've made it up again!' shouts Jip. And he gives Janneke a kiss.

'That's right,' says Janneke. 'It's all over.' And they link arms.

Off they go. They'll be staying away for a long time. And they wave again to all the children. To you too. Wave back.

Bye, Jip!

Bye, Janneke!

Other books by Annie M.G. Schmidt and Fiep Westendorp

For more than fifty years, Jip and Janneke have been the Netherlands' favourite and most famous preschoolers. They are best friends who play together, argue, get into mischief and eat too many sweets. Even modern children have no trouble identifying with these timeless adventures.

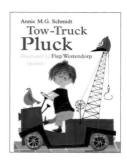

There's a room free in the Pill Building. Up on top, in the tower. When Pluck finds out, he drives straight there in his red tow truck. Finally he has a home. And right away he makes lots of new friends: Zaza the cockroach and Dolly the pigeon, Mr Penn, the Stampers and Aggie. Pluck's adventures can begin.

A flippable book with two stories about Scrumple and her dog Splotch. Scrumple gets very, very dirty and badly needs a bath. A bath with bubbles, lots and lots of bubbles...

www.annie-mg.com
www.fiepwestendorp.nl
www.jipenjanneke.nl
www.queridokinderboeken.nl

The stories and black-and-white illustrations in this book first appeared in the 1950s in the newspaper *Het Parool* and have long counted as classics in Flanders and the Netherlands. Fiep Westendorp did the additional colour illustrations in the late seventies for *Bobo*, a magazine for preschoolers.

Original title: *Met Jip en Janneke door Nederland* (Querido, 2014)

Cover illustrations Fiep Westendorp
Design Irma Hornman, Studio Cursief

ISBN 978 90 451 2058 4 / NUR 281